IST GRADE DINOSAUR BOOK
NAME THAT DINOSAUR

SPEEDY
PUBLISHING

Speedy Publishing LLC
40 E. Main St. #1156
Newark, DE 19711
www.speedypublishing.com

Dinosaurs first appeared around 231.4 million years ago. They were the dominant terrestrial vertebrates for 135 million years.

Tyrannosaurus rex is often abbreviated to T-Rex. The Tyrannosaurus rex was one of the largest land predator dinosaurs.

The T-rex measured up to 43 feet long and weighed as much as 7.5 tons.

The Velociraptor was a fairly small dinosaur. It was around 6 feet long and weighed around 30 pounds.

Velociraptor lived around 73 million years ago. The Velociraptor lived in a desert like environment.

Spinosaurus is best known for its tall, thin back spines. The Spinosaurus had powerful jaws with straight teeth.

Fossils of the Spinosaurus were first found in Egypt around 1910.

Triceratops means three-horned face. Triceratops was the largest of the horned dinosaurs.

It is believed that fully grown Triceratops were about 8m in length. The Triceratops was a herbivore.

The Stegosaurus is most famous for the diamond shaped plates that are lined up and down its back.

The Stegosaurus was large and heavily built. Stegosaurus had brains the size of ping pong balls.

Diplodocus lived in an area that is now western North America at the end of the Jurassic Period.

Diplodocus had a 26 foot long neck and a 45 foot long, whip-like tail.

Apatosaurus lived in the Jurassic Period, around 150 million years ago. The Apatosaurus was a herbivore.

The Apatosaurus is one of the largest animals to ever live on earth.

The Allosaurus may have been the most fearsome meat-eating dinosaur of the Mesozoic Era.

Allosaurus had a large skull and walked on two legs. Allosaurus was up to 39 feet long, and weighed approximately 1.7 tons.

The Brachiosaurus had a long neck, a small head and a relatively short tail. These dinosaurs were herbivores.

The Brachiosaurus walked on all four legs. The brachiosaurus' front legs are longer than its hind legs.

65864141R00024

Made in the USA
Middletown, DE
05 March 2018